973
POR

Colorado

c/

Steck-Vaughn Company
Executive Editor	Diane Sharpe
Senior Editor	Martin S. Saiewitz
Design Manager	Pamela Heaney
Photo Editor	Margie Foster

Proof Positive/Farrowlyne Associates, Inc.
Program Editorial, Revision Development, Design, and Production

Consultant: University of Colorado at Boulder

Published by Raintree Steck-Vaughn Publishers, an imprint of Steck-Vaughn Company.

A Turner Educational Services, Inc. book. Based on the Portrait of America television series by R. E. (Ted) Turner.

Cover Photo: Dunsinane and Precipice Peaks by © Larry Ulrich/Tony Stone Images.

Library of Congress Cataloging-in-Publication Data

Thompson, Kathleen.
    Colorado / Kathleen Thompson.
        p.   cm. — (Portrait of America)
    "A Turner book."
    "Based on the Portrait of America television series"—T.p. verso.
    Includes index.
    ISBN 0-8114-7326-0 (library binding).—ISBN 0-8114-7431-3 (softcover)
    1. Colorado—Juvenile literature. [1. Colorado.] I. Title.
    II. Series: Thompson, Kathleen. Portrait of America.
    F776.3.T46   1996
    978.8—dc20   95-40010
                                                                    CIP
                                                                    AC

Acknowledgments
The publishers wish to thank the following for permission to reproduce photographs:
P. 7 © Michael Reagan; p. 8 © M. Gaede/Museum of Northern Arizona; pp. 10, 11, 12, 14, 15, 16 Colorado Historical Society; p. 17 U.S. Air Force Photograph, Peterson AFB, Colorado; p. 18 The Western Sugar Company; p. 19 Denver International Airport; pp. 20, 21, 22, 23 U.S. Senator Ben Nighthorse Campbell; p. 24 © John Elk/Tony Stone Images; p. 26 © Biege Jones Photo, Aspen Skiing Company; p. 27 © David Steinke/USDA Forest Service; p. 28 U.S. Air Force Photograph, U.S. Air Force Academy, Colorado; p. 29 Martin Marietta Astronautics Group; p. 30 (bottom) © Michael Reagan, (top) © Ken Missbrenner; p. 31 © Michael Reagan; p. 32 © Superstock; p. 34 Denver Convention and Visitors Bureau; p. 35 (top) © Amos Cordova/Durango & Silverton Narrow Gauge Railroad, (bottom) Central City Opera; p. 36 © Gregg Adams Photo, Aspen Skiing Company; p. 37 (top) © Robert Biddlecome/Aspen Music Festival, (bottom) © Larry Pierce/Steamboat Ski Company; p. 38 © Michael Reagan; p. 39 (top) © Baxter Black, (bottom) © Scott O'Malley & Associates; p. 40 © Michael Reagan; p. 41 (top) © Michael Reagan, (bottom) Colorado Convention & Visitors Bureau; p. 42 © Superstock; p. 44 © Burnham Arndt Photo, Aspen Skiing Company; p. 46 One Mile Up; p. 47 (left) One Mile Up, (center) © Vireo, (right) Texas Wildflower Research Center.

STECK-VAUGHN
PORTRAIT OF AMERICA

Colorado

Kathleen Thompson

A Turner Book

RAINTREE
STECK-VAUGHN
PUBLISHERS
The Steck-Vaughn Company

Austin, Texas

Colorado

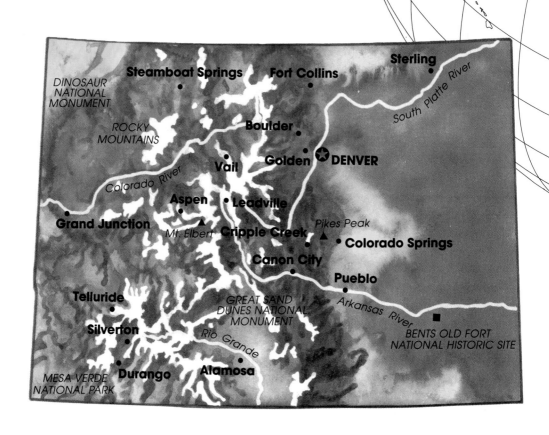

Sterling

Steamboat Springs

Fort Collins

DINOSAUR
NATIONAL
MONUMENT

South Platte River

ROCKY
MOUNTAINS

Boulder

Vail

Golden

DENVER

Colorado River

Aspen

Leadville

Grand Junction

Mt. Elbert

Cripple Creek

Pikes Peak

Colorado Springs

Canon City

Pueblo

Telluride

GREAT SAND
DUNES NATIONAL
MONUMENT

Arkansas River

Silverton

Rio Grande

BENTS OLD FORT
NATIONAL HISTORIC SITE

Durango

Alamosa

MESA VERDE
NATIONAL PARK

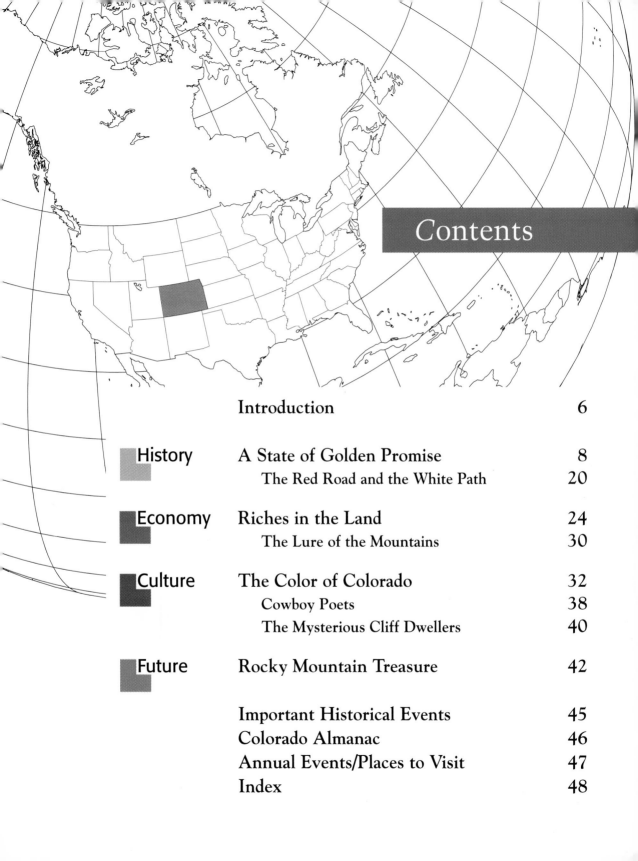

Contents

Introduction

When you think of outdoors, mountain peaks, and mile-high living, Colorado should come to mind. This state has world-class views and high-class entertainment. In summer the Rocky Mountains attract hikers, campers, and cyclists. Colorado's famous ski resorts keep people outdoors all winter long. But Colorado is more than a playground. People also earn their living farming and mining the land, just as the original pioneers who settled there did. The state's location—halfway between the Midwest and the West Coast—has brought high-tech businesses to the mountains, too. Colorado has set its sights on the twenty-first century and is taking its pioneer pride along with it.

Colorado's Rocky Mountains are young for a mountain range—only 30 million to 65 million years old. Their tops are still sharp and jagged because they haven't been worn down by time.

Colorado

A State of Golden Promise

Native Americans have been living in the area now known as Colorado since prehistoric times. Arrowheads dating back more than ten thousand years have been discovered throughout the state. Native Americans made tools from stone and bones, hunted mammals, and gathered seeds, nuts, and roots.

The region was occupied much later by cliff dwellers who built warm and comfortable homes inside caves. The Navajo, who came to live in the area centuries later, called these people the *Anasazi*, which means "ancient ones." Archaeologists also called them the Basket Makers because they made finely crafted baskets that we still find today. The Anasazi occupied present-day Colorado and the surrounding states to the Southwest from 100 B.C. to A.D. 1200. These people developed large, impressive multilevel cliff dwellings. Toward the end of the thirteenth century, the Anasazi joined other Native American groups. These groups, now known as the Pueblo, included Hopi and Zuni.

This Hopi woman is making pottery. When the pot is shaped, she will decorate it with a traditional design and bake it in a coal-fired oven.

The first Europeans to enter new territories in northeastern North America were usually the English or the French. But farther west it was the Spaniards who came north from Mexico. These explorers often were looking only for gold, not new land to settle. When they found no gold, they simply moved on, never to return.

The Spanish explorer Francisco Vásquez de Coronado passed through the Colorado area in the early 1500s. He and his group were returning from a journey that took them from Mexico into Kansas. Much later, in 1706 a Spanish official named Juan de Ulibarri came to eastern Colorado. He claimed the area for Spain. For the next 140 years, Spain, Mexico, and finally the United States all made claims to the Colorado region.

The United States bought a large part of Colorado in the Louisiana Purchase of 1803. The purchase was a land deal that President Thomas Jefferson made with Napoleon Bonaparte, then emperor of France. Napoleon needed money to finance his European wars. France had claim to all the land in the Mississippi River Valley, and Napoleon sold that claim to the United States. The purchase greatly increased the size of the new United States and included what is now eastern and central Colorado.

American explorers began to come into Colorado as a result of the Louisiana Purchase. The most famous of these was Zebulon M. Pike. He arrived in the area in 1806 and gave his name to a magnificent 14,110-foot-high mountain, Pikes Peak. Other expeditions that

Zebulon M. Pike was one of the first United States explorers to enter what is now Colorado, but he never climbed the mountain that bears his name.

Standing majestically alone, Pikes Peak was a landmark that guided the pioneers as they journeyed west.

explored the Colorado mountains included those of Major Stephen H. Long and John C. Frémont. Long also named a mountain, Long's Peak, after himself. Eventually trappers and fur traders known as "mountain men" settled in the area. In 1833 trader William Bent founded Bent's Fort, the first permanent settlement in Colorado. The famous scout Kit Carson was chief hunter there. His job was to provide the people of Bent's Fort with meat from the wild animals in the area.

In 1821 after an 11-year fight for independence, Mexico won its freedom from Spain. This meant that Mexico now owned the former Spanish territory. Some of this territory was in what is now the southwestern United States. In 1846 the United States and Mexico went to war. They fought over territory that both sides claimed was theirs. The war lasted less than two years,

A miner pans for gold in a Colorado stream. Many sought the precious metal, but only a few struck it rich.

and United States troops won every battle. When the final treaty was signed in February 1848, the United States had won vast Mexican holdings that covered parts of what later became eight states, including western Colorado.

The trappers and traders who came to Bent's Fort—people like Kit Carson and Jim Bridger—had no interest in settling the land. Like the Spanish, they were after quick money. In their case, it was the money they could get by selling beaver fur. People weren't interested in settling the land until 1858. That was the year prospectors found the gold the Spanish had been looking for.

Suddenly, hundreds of covered wagons and thousands of gold hunters headed for Colorado. The miners quickly moved from one gold strike to the next. New camps and mining towns sprang up almost overnight. Settlers established mining camps in such places as Central City, Gold Hill, Boulder, and Cripple Creek.

The miners were sure that they would make their fortunes in the hills of Colorado. A few of them did, but most found only hardship and disappointment. In spite of this, many of them stayed and began raising crops and livestock. About a year after the first cry of "Gold!" went up, there were one hundred thousand people in Colorado.

However, there was a problem. The settlers were on land that had been guaranteed in treaties to Native Americans by the United States government. But the settlers paid no attention to the claims on the land. They ruled themselves. What justice there was in the area was handed out by people's courts. At that time Colorado was part of the area Congress called the Kansas Territory. But with their newfound wealth, the settlers wanted their own political identity. In 1859 they met in convention and declared that the area would be called the Jefferson Territory. However, Congress paid no attention to this illegal government. In 1861 Congress created the Colorado Territory.

In 1862 oil was discovered. Also, new methods of ore processing made it practical to reopen mines that had been thought to be exhausted. Silver was discovered, bringing a new mining boom. By the 1870s the Colorado Territory was prospering. Farms and ranches were becoming larger and more productive. Colorado became the thirty-eighth state on August 1, 1876. Its nickname, "The Centennial State," comes from the fact that it attained statehood one hundred years after the 13 colonies declared their independence from Great Britain.

In the meantime Native Americans in Colorado were fighting unsuccessfully for their lands. The Cheyenne and Arapaho were told by the United

Ouray the Arrow, leader of the Ute, is shown with his wife, Chipeta. When Ouray died in 1880, no new leader took over the struggle.

This train is traveling on the Argentine Central Railroad—in Colorado, not South America. Builders laid track through valleys and on mountainsides and tunneled through mountains too high to cross.

States government that they must live within an approved boundary. After a few years, Native Americans refused to stay on their piece of land. Settlers poured onto Native American lands, then called on the government and the Colorado militia to protect them. In 1864 the Colorado militia attacked the Cheyenne and Arapaho at Sand Creek as they were trying to surrender. Three hundred Native American men, women, and children were killed in the massacre. Congress appointed a committee to investigate and eventually paid the Cheyenne for their loss. The battles with the Arapaho, Cheyenne, and

During the 1930s, farms in the Great Plains were ruined by droughts and dust storms. Millions of tons of topsoil were blown away, and thousands of farm families went bankrupt.

Ute, which had continued through the 1860s and 1870s, came to an end in 1880. A treaty was signed in 1881, resulting in Native Americans being removed to reservations.

The new state was an exciting, colorful place for the others who lived there then. The mines brought in money, and the miners spent it. When the price of silver dropped, prospectors began mining other mineral resources, such as coal, oil, and molybdenum, which is used in making steel. The Union Pacific Railroad, which linked California to the East, made Denver an important shipping point. Iron production began, and factories were built. During this time, however, improved irrigation methods made farming the dominant source of Colorado's economy. One of the major crops was sugar beets. The first sugar refinery in the state opened in 1899.

In the 1930s the country fell into the Great Depression. Banks and factories closed, and hundreds of thousands of people were out of work. The problem became worse in Colorado when a bad drought fell upon the state's eastern plains. The drought lasted from 1932 to 1937, and the area became part of what was known as the "Dust Bowl." As in the rest of the nation, strong government programs brought some relief to Colorado. However, it was not until the United States became involved in World War II that Colorado's economy recovered completely. Many of the state's products were needed for the war effort. Also, the United States government set up several military bases in Colorado.

After the war, the population of the state began to grow rapidly. Colorado has had the most rapid population growth among the mountain states. Before World War II, in 1940, there were about 1.2 million people living in Colorado, about 52 percent of them in the

These satellite-systems operators are controlling satellites from Falcon Air Force Base.

cities. By 1960 there were more than 1.75 million people in the state. Almost seventy percent of them lived in the three largest cities. This rapid increase in urban population, however, put a severe burden on the state's modest water supplies. Colorado uses most of its water supply for irrigated agriculture. Since the early 1950s, a series of dams, tunnels, and reservoirs have been built to ensure that Colorado farmland gets enough water. In 1962 a three-dam system now known as the Wayne N. Aspinall Storage Unit was begun. In 1985 the Frying Pan-Arkansas Project, which transfers water across the state, was completed.

Another one of Colorado's biggest concerns in the last few decades of the twentieth century has been air and water pollution. An additional problem is waste

A farmer is harvesting sugar beets. The sugar beet became a major crop in the late 1800s, and it still is an important part of Colorado agriculture.

Denver International Airport opened in 1995, replacing Denver's Stapleton International Airport. Denver's airport is the sixth busiest in the country.

disposal for the people living on the eastern slopes of the Rockies. This area houses more than three fourths of the state's population. Finally, the huge number of tourists threatens to harm the very wilderness the people come to see.

Even with these problems, however, Colorado is a thriving state. People come from all over the country, even the world, to enjoy its open-air beauty. Its farms are rich and fruitful. Denver has become one of the country's largest and most important centers of arts, commerce, and sports. Long after the Spanish explorers gave up their search for gold, Colorado has fulfilled its golden promise.

The Red Road and the White Path

Ben Nighthorse Campbell looks at the Colorado land around him with Native American eyes. He is part of a civilization that has lost most of its power, and he knows that all things—made by people as well as by nature—are subject to change. "They say six civilizations have lived in this part of Colorado," says Mr. Campbell. "Well, we know the people who lived here in

Senator Campbell rides in traditional tribal costume. He is a chief of the Northern Cheyenne.

these rocks and in these cliffs were here twice as long, or more, than the United States has been a country. Children being born and men dying of old age. And you are just a little piece in that structure, in that passing of time."

Ben Nighthorse Campbell was born in 1933 in California. His mother was a Portuguese immigrant, and his father was a Northern Cheyenne. All his life, Mr. Campbell has lived in the two worlds represented by his parents. He never lost contact with his Cheyenne heritage. Today, he is a member of the Council of 44 Chiefs of the Northern Cheyenne Tribe centered in Lame Deer, Montana.

Ben Nighthorse Campbell went to college in California and Japan. He studied the martial art of judo, and three times he was the United States judo champion. He won a gold medal in judo at the 1963 Pan-American Games, and he has served as a coach for the United States international judo team. In 1964 he was captain of the United States judo team that competed at the Tokyo Olympic Games.

Ben Nighthorse Campbell may be the only United States senator who rides a Harley-Davidson motorcycle.

After college he went on to become a successful businessman. As a self-employed jewelry designer, he has won more than two hundred first-place and best-of-show awards. He was also a rancher and has trained champion quarter horses.

His success continued when he entered politics. Mr. Campbell was first elected to the Colorado state legislature in 1982 and served four years. In 1986 he was voted one of the ten best senators in the state by his colleagues.

21

Mr. Campbell served in the United States House of Representatives from 1987 to 1992. In November 1992 he was elected to the United States Senate. He was the first Native American senator in more than sixty years. Currently he is the only Native American in either the House or the Senate.

Mr. Campbell is aware that as a person with a heritage that is both Native American and European, "You have to be very sensitive to both worlds and what we call the red road or the white path. People tend to want to push you into categories like that."

Mr. Campbell feels that the only way Native Americans can live in twentieth century America without losing their roots is to follow both ways, to go the "red road" and follow the "white path."

As a senator, Mr. Campbell represents all the people of Colorado. His special concerns, however, are for Native Americans and their problems and for the preservation of the natural outdoors. He helped pass important laws to settle Native American water rights, and he has sponsored other laws to protect Colorado wilderness areas and water resources. He is very sensitive to the balance between public land use and the need to preserve the land.

Mr. Campbell stresses the fact that Native American traditions and culture are alive and well. He is concerned that for many years many school textbooks did not include information on Native American culture.

Here is a necklace made by Ben Nighthorse Campbell. Robert Redford and Paul Newman are among the many famous people who proudly wear his "Painted Mesa" jewelry.

"Fortunately, more and more books are coming out by Native American authors," Mr. Campbell said. "People are learning more about what . . . we're like today."

Ben Nighthorse Campbell also fights for Native Americans of the past. For example, he worked hard to change the name of the Custer Battlefield Monument in Montana to the Little Bighorn National Monument. He wanted the name of the monument to reflect the bravery of all the men who fought and died there, not just the soldiers who fought on General George Custer's side. The name was changed in 1991. Mr. Campbell has also worked to create a National Museum of the American Indian within the Smithsonian Institution.

He knows that changes like these will give young Native Americans added pride in their heritage. He also knows that this pride is desperately needed.

Fortunately, there's another side to the picture, and the gradually improving life for Native Americans gives Mr. Campbell hope for the future. He feels that there are many more opportunities now for Native Americans. Many

Senator Campbell began his career of national service early in life. He served in the Korean War as a member of the United States Air Force.

are doctors, lawyers, and teachers—people who have degrees and professions. "Those are the ones who are [telling] youngsters on the reservations: 'You can make it. Have faith in yourself. You can do it.' That's made a big impact," Mr. Campbell said.

Today, no one is a more visible role model for those youngsters than Ben Nighthorse Campbell—a Native American chief *and* a United States senator. He is living proof that a person can walk both the red road and the white path.

Riches in the Land

Six of this country's major rivers begin in Colorado. That's an amazing number for one state. Yet, from the very beginning of its development as an agricultural area, Colorado has had water problems. The biggest problem was how to get the water from where it fell as rain to the fields where it was needed. Most of the state's rainfall is on the western side of the Rockies, and most of the usable farm land is on the eastern side. But another problem developed later.

The rivers that begin in Colorado flow through many states. The United States Supreme Court has decided that the water from those rivers has to be divided fairly among the states the rivers flow through. One result is that Colorado has been in more court cases about water use than any other state. It also has made agreements with nearby states and Mexico about how much water can be used by each.

Colorado has many reservoirs for storing water, tunnels for carrying it, and dams for irrigation and flood control. This means that the eastern side of

Logs are a practical building material for people who live in Colorado, since about one third of Colorado is forested.

A skier zooms down a steep slope near Aspen. More than 35 major ski areas make Colorado a haven for winter sports enthusiasts.

Colorado has flourishing farmlands and busy factories that are kept going, in part, on water from the western side. Several long tunnels actually have been dug through the Rocky Mountains to bring the precious water to where it is most needed.

It was gold that first brought people to Colorado. But irrigated farmland soon made agriculture the state's largest industry. In addition, vast herds of cattle grazed the land where buffalo once roamed. Colorado became one of the nation's leading meat producers. Plant crops and meat production led the state's economy until the early years of the twentieth century. Then, in 1954 manufacturing of machinery, electrical products, and military hardware moved into first place.

Today, as in most states, service industries account for a very large part of Colorado's income. Service industries are those in which people don't manufacture an actual product. Instead they may work at a department store, a bank, or an insurance company. In Colorado, nearly four fifths of the annual gross state product—the total yearly value of all the goods and services produced in the state—comes from service industries.

Manufacturing brings in about ten percent of Colorado's income. The largest part of that comes from scientific instruments, medical equipment, and devices that measure electricity. The second biggest kind of manufacturing in Colorado is food processing. In addition to meat products, the state also is a leading producer of beer, soft drinks, and animal feeds. Nonelectrical machinery, once the state's leading product, is far less important today. Still Colorado's factories produce many kinds of machines used in construction and farming. Computers and consumer electronics are produced in Colorado also. Televisions, telephones, and camcorders are playing an ever-larger role in the state's economy.

Agriculture accounts for about three percent of Colorado's gross state product. Colorado has about 27,000 farms. These vary in size from huge ranches to small truck farms where one family grows vegetables to sell. Beef cattle are the single most important agricultural product. The largest field crops are hay, wheat, corn, and sugar beets. Colorado farms and orchards also produce many kinds of vegetables and fruits, especially apples.

About two percent of the gross state product of Colorado comes from mining. At one time, of course, precious metals, such as silver and gold, were the state's

These cattle are being rounded up at Union Park. More than forty percent of Colorado is pastureland, and beef cattle are the state's major agricultural product.

most valuable mineral products. Today, that honor is held by fuels such as petroleum, natural gas, and coal.

During the 1950s and 1960s, uranium deposits in southwestern Colorado played an important role in the state's mining operations. Until a few years ago, the United States was manufacturing great numbers of atomic weapons and constructing nuclear power plants. Modern-day prospectors scoured the hills for traces of the precious metal. They rode jeeps instead of burros and used Geiger counters instead of gold pans. But their "strike it rich" mentality was the same as that of the gold prospectors a century before.

Today, production of atomic weapons has almost stopped. Also, very few new nuclear power plants are being built, so the demand for uranium is much reduced. But most of the uranium used in the United States still comes from Colorado.

Military bases have been set up in Colorado since World War II. They were located in Colorado to be far enough from either coast to be safe from any possible invasion. The army opened Fort Carson near Colorado Springs and a huge ammunition plant at Pueblo.

Today, government provides about 14 percent of Colorado's gross state product. Part of that comes from state and local governments, but the federal government plays a major role. The Air Force operates the Air Force Academy in Colorado Springs and the North American Aerospace Defense Command (NORAD) near the academy.

The military's presence in the area has attracted many companies that manufacture military equipment

The Air Force Academy opened near Colorado Springs in 1958. Part of the training is learning to pilot gliders.

and supplies. From the 1950s until the early 1990s, Colorado companies produced missiles, atomic warheads, and many other items used in war. Today, two major satellite manufacturers and two companies that make booster rockets for satellite launches are located in Colorado.

Since the turn of the century, ever-increasing numbers of tourists have brought money into Colorado. Now tourism adds $6.4 billion a year, or $17 million a day, to the state's economy. More than nine percent of all jobs are related to tourism.

Colorado provides a wide variety of recreational opportunities. It is best known as a winter ski area. The oldest and largest resorts are at Aspen and Vail, but new areas have been opening almost yearly. Today, Colorado has 27 major resort areas, some with dozens of ski runs.

Summer also attracts vacationers by the millions. Colorado averages three hundred sunny days a year. This is more than the average for either San Diego or Miami. Summer activities include whitewater rafting, playing golf, wind-surfing, mountain biking, hot-air ballooning, hiking, and camping.

The explorers of old went to Colorado to find the gold they were sure was there. Today's Colorado businesses only have to make the state's beauty accessible and comfortable . . . and tourists bring the "gold" to them!

In the Martin Marietta Company's Space Operations Simulation Lab, models demonstrate space-ship motions in zero gravity.

The Lure of the Mountains

It seems that wherever you go in Colorado, you are surrounded by nature. It's not surprising that many Colorado residents get into the wilderness whenever they can. The call of the wild is difficult to resist. The earliest explorers and mountain men followed it into uncharted territory. Modern Coloradans hear it, too.

These ski patrol members are rescuing an injured skier.

On rescue missions, Debbie Hutchinson works with a dog who is trained to dig out skiers who are buried under the snow.

"When the winds are so strong that they close down the lifts and everything, I think it's great that nature is that powerful. Sometimes I don't always want to be out in it, but I like it. . . . That's one of the reasons why I'm up here."

Debbie Hutchinson is a member of the ski patrol. She is one of the people whose job is to make sure that skiers don't get lost or hurt on the slopes. Members of the ski patrol have to know the mountains and the outdoors in general, and Debbie does. "This is a good job for me," she says. "I'm happy. And that's all that counts."

Stuart Mace, who spent more than forty years taking visitors on guided tours of the mountain back country by dog sled, also heard the call of the mountains.

"Before the war I had the privilege of climbing all the 14,000-foot peaks on the North American continent," Mace said. "So I had a lot of snow and cold and a lot of mountain. My heart's been in the mountains anyhow. The people who used to live here, people they call mountain people, lived in harmony and balance with this land."

More and more people are following the call of the mountains. But so many people visit Colorado's lovely wilderness areas that they may be destroying the very beauty they came to find. Both the state and federal governments try to protect the land by only letting a limited number of people enter certain areas. Littering and land-use rules are strictly enforced. Even picking wildflowers is not allowed in many places. "Take nothing but photographs; leave nothing but your footprints" is the motto of responsible nature lovers.

Even if you never go to the mountains, there's lots to do outdoors in Colorado. Water sports are very popular. Locals and tourists float down rivers and whitewater streams in rafts, canoes, and kayaks. Those with a taste for a more difficult water sport enjoy windsurfing. There are even sailing races on Colorado's larger lakes.

In Telluride during June, dozens of brightly colored globes fill the clear mountain sky during the annual hot-air balloon rally. One of the most important events in the sport, the rally draws participants from all over the world. On land, on water, and even in the air, Colorado offers an endless variety of outdoor pleasures.

Stuart Mace lives among the mountains he loves in a Castle Creek Valley log cabin.

31

The Color of Colorado

In Spanish the name *Colorado* means "colored red." If you were looking for one place typical of Colorado culture, you couldn't do better than Red Rocks. In a mountain park outside Denver, this natural outdoor theater, or amphitheater, seats nine thousand people.

Most people who visit pack a big picnic lunch. They drive out of Denver and through the foothills of the Rockies to the park. Even on bright, sunny afternoons, there's a slight chill in the clear mountain air. It's perfect for playing in the outdoors.

After a picnic supper, it's cool enough for a sweater, even in June or July. Gradually, the amphitheater fills up as people find places on the red rock seats. They might hear a world-famous musician, a popular singer, or an opera. In many ways, it's the perfect mix of the outdoors and high-quality culture.

That's the way life seems to work in Colorado. People spend as much of it as they can outdoors. They go to the mountains; they camp, hike, fish, and hunt.

These kids are downhill skiing in Steamboat Springs, Colorado. Over 15 million Americans enjoy downhill or cross-country skiing. Colorado is the most popular state for skiing in the United States.

The Denver Art Museum has paintings by Degas, Monet, and Picasso in its collection.

But they care about—and support—a wide range of institutions and activities. For example, Denver has an art museum, a symphony orchestra, and a civic theater, as well as both history and natural history museums. Central City has a fine old opera house. It was built back in the silver boom days of the last century, and it's still used for both opera and theater. Colorado Springs is proud of its Fine Arts Center.

Even away from the main population centers, Colorado residents are proud of their culture and heritage. Throughout the state there are more than

The Durango & Silverton narrow-gauge train crawls along the wall of the Animas River Canyon. The ride offers spectacular mountain views and is a popular tourist attraction.

The Central City Opera House was built more than a century ago at the height of Colorado's silver boom.

one hundred museums and zoos. Many of the museums have an Old West theme and feature Native American traditions, pioneer life, and military history. They also give much information about the mines and railroads that brought so much wealth to Colorado. One of the most interesting museums is the Colorado Railroad Museum in Golden.

However, Colorado is so beautiful that most people prefer to stay in the open air. So, as in Red Rocks, they try to combine culture and nature. One of the most successful examples of this happens in Aspen, which is a world-famous ski center in winter. Each summer the town hosts a unique festival of music, cultural studies, and outdoor activities. In other parts of the state, you'll find rodeos, boat races, and dozens of summer festivals.

Tourists spend a great deal of time enjoying the wonders of two national parks, six national monuments, a national historic site, a national historic area, and twelve national forests. The federal government owns one third of all the land in Colorado. Adding to this wealth of outdoor possibilities are 35 state parks and numerous federal and state recreation areas. So, no matter how many museums you visit or concerts you attend, in Colorado you're never far from the unspoiled beauty of nature.

The Winterskol festivals at Aspen and Snowmass ski areas last an entire week.

Although famous for its skiing, Aspen is also well known for its summer activities. Music Associates of Aspen presents the Aspen Music Festival every summer, and Ballet/Aspen holds a dance festival.

A balloon rally in Steamboat Springs fills the air with silently floating lighter-than-air craft.

Cowboy Poets

"Son, he'd say,
You'll never have any pride
If you don't get up right now
And finish the ride."

Cowboy poet Nyle Henderson describes in verse growing up on a Colorado ranch and the western way of life.

Nyle Henderson breaks horses on Colorado ranches for a living. So he knows how it feels to get thrown off and get back on. He also writes poetry. Communicating the kind of life he lives, and how he feels about things, is very important to him. He knows that when his father insisted that he get back on a horse that had thrown him, he was telling his son about life.

"He wasn't just talking
About a horse that could buck,
He was talking about any
    problems
I might try to duck."

Nyle is just one of a new breed of "cowboy poets" who are carrying on one of the oldest traditions of the West. The European fascination with poetry went west with the pioneers. By the time of the great cattle drives in the 1870s and 1880s, cowboys were sharing rhyming poems around their campfires.

Today, several hundred of these poets are scattered across the West, mostly working on ranches. Very few are famous. Former talk-show host Johnny Carson is a fan of cowboy poetry, however, and he had several of the poets on his show.

Waddie Mitchell, a working cowboy for almost thirty years, says, "I grew up on my Dad's ranch thirty miles by dirt road from the nearest town. We had no electricity and no television. I didn't even know who Johnny Carson was when he invited me for my first appearance!"

Colorado's Baxter Black worked for years as a veterinarian before his poetry made him famous enough to have a program on National Public Radio. He also writes a weekly newspaper humor column called "On the Edge of Common Sense." The poems in it poke fun at everything from vegetarians to the problems ranchers have trying to get a loan at a bank.

Baxter is one of the few cowboy poets who earns any money from his verse. Most do it just for their own

Baxter Black, shown here with his dog, often performs at the annual Cowboy Poetry Gathering. He also writes agricultural columns, practices veterinary medicine, and reads humorous poems over the air for National Public Radio.

enjoyment and the pleasure of those who listen. Some even refuse to write their poems down. "It just doesn't work on paper," insists Wally McRae, a spirited performer whose work might best be called "cowboy rap."

Like many other old-time traditions, the century-old craft of cowboy poetry is alive and flourishing.

Waddie Mitchell (right) has appeared on The Tonight Show *four times. He travels three hundred days out of the year, earning between $2,500 and $10,000 per performance.*

The Mysterious Cliff Dwellers

At Mesa Verde National Park, you can see the remains of an ancient civilization. Most of their dwellings were built on cliff ledges. The people made them out of sandstone bricks and mud mortar. Other dwellings were carved out of the sheer rock face of the mountainside. Who were these cliff dwellers? They were Native Americans the Navajo later called the Anasazi, or "the ancient ones." To find proof of their ancient way of life, you need look no farther than Mesa Verde National Park.

The park, located in southwestern Colorado, was founded in 1906 to preserve the cliff dwellings there. Scientists believe that the Anasazi built most of their mud and mortar homes in the 1200s. Some of these dwellings were three and four stories high. Thick walls kept the dwellings cool in summer while protecting against the elements all year long. Several of these cliff dwellings have more than two hundred rooms. Some of these rooms are *kivas,* circular rooms that were used for religious ceremonies. The lower floors of these structures had no doors. Residents had to climb ladders to reach doors in the upper levels. Then, once they were inside, they could descend

There was no standard plan to the buildings at Mesa Verde. The Anasazi fitted the buildings to the space that was available.

In Spanish, mesa verde *means "green table." The land above the cliff dwellings was flat, forming a kind of green table on which the Anasazi grew crops.*

to the lower rooms. In case of attack, the outside ladders could be pulled up to create a safe refuge.

Just who were the Anasazi? Why did they live on the sides of mountains instead of in the valley? How long did it take them to build their massive multiroom dwellings? Historians have puzzled over these questions for a long time. That's because the Anasazi left no written record of their culture. The centuries-old ruins show that the people were skilled builders. There is also evidence that the Anasazi were farmers. They were able to grow corn, beans, and other crops in the dry land at the base of the cliffs. Archaeologists have also found fragments of weapons, pottery, and baskets made by the Anasazi. Because of these facts, archaeologists have placed the Anasazi among the most advanced ancient cultures in North America.

By the year 1300, nearly all of the Anasazi had abandoned their cliff dwellings. Some scholars believe that a long drought forced them to move. We may never know whether or not that was the reason. The true answer may remain, like the Anasazi themselves, wrapped in mystery.

To build the cliff houses, the Anasazi used only stone, bone, and wood tools. They are considered a Stone Age people because they had no metal.

Rocky Mountain Treasure

To some people, Colorado seems like paradise—or the nearest thing to it. It has towering peaks and crisp mountain air. Signs of its colorful history are everywhere—mine shacks still dot the mountainside, and remnants of the Anasazi culture that are twenty centuries old line the red-rock cliffs.

However, no place is perfect, and Colorado does have some problems. They do not show at first glance. Most of them have been caused by people wanting the benefits of twentieth-century technology.

The crisp mountain air has been polluted by industry. The sparkling rivers and streams have been dulled by industrial waste. The waters have been poisoned by the careless mining practices of the past. The eastern slope of the Rockies, where four fifths of the state's people live, is suffering from massive overcrowding. Water is often in short supply, even with all the tunnels and aqueducts that have been built to carry it from the other side of the mountains.

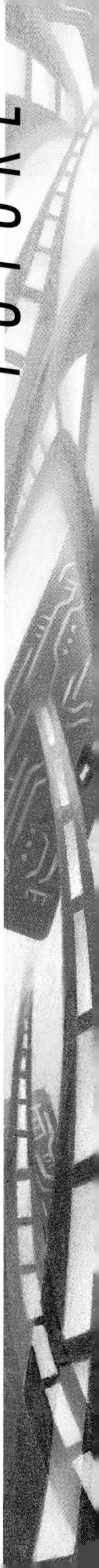

Denver is the commercial center for the Rocky Mountain region. The 16th Street Mall in downtown Denver, shown here, is 14 city blocks long.

For skiers in Aspen, like many other Coloradans and visitors, fun in the scenic outdoors is an important part of their lives.

Colorado's economy has been hurt since the government has cut back on defense spending. Traditionally, the military and defense contractors have been two of the state's major sources of jobs and revenue. With less money going in that direction, Colorado must attract or develop new kinds of business and industry.

Even though Colorado is not paradise, it is still a place where people value the beauty of the land around them. In the years since pollution has been recognized as a serious problem, Colorado has received some assistance in protecting the outdoors. The National Weather Service and the Solar Energy Research Institute are both looking for energy sources that will not damage the air, water, or soil.

The beauty of Colorado is worth working to save. The people of Colorado realize this. True, the state is not perfect. But it is a wonderful example of people working to enjoy the benefits of modern life amid the beauty of nature.

Important Historical Events

100 B.C.	Anasazi Basket Makers live in caves in the area that will become Colorado.
A.D. 1300	The Pueblo establish farms in the Colorado area.
1540	The Cheyenne, Arapaho, and Ute live in the area when Francisco Vasquez de Coronado reaches the southwest corner.
1706	Juan de Ulibarri enters eastern Colorado and claims it for Spain.
1776	Franciscan missionaries Francisco Vélez Sivestre de Escalante and Francisco Dominguez cross present-day western Colorado.
1803	The Louisiana Purchase is completed. The eastern portion of present-day Colorado is included in the purchase.
1806	Zebulon M. Pike explores the Colorado area.
1819	Spain gives to the United States the area north of the Arkansas River in present-day Colorado.
1820	Stephen H. Long explores the Colorado area.
1833	Bent's Fort is established on the Arkansas River.
1842	John C. Frémont begins his exploration of the Colorado area.
1848	Mexico gives up western Colorado to the United States as part of the treaty that ended the Mexican War.
1858	Green Russell discovers gold in Colorado, starting a gold rush.
1859	Denver, Black Hawk, Golden, Central City, Mount Vernon, and Nevadaville are all founded.

1861	The Colorado Territory is established by the United States Congress.
1864	Colorado militia attack a Cheyenne village at Sand Creek and murder three hundred people in what has come to be called the Sand Creek Massacre.
1870	The Union Pacific Railroad makes Denver an important depot.
1876	Colorado is admitted into the Union, becoming the 38th state.
1890 to 1900	There are serious troubles between miners and mine owners. Martial law is declared several times.
1915	Rocky Mountain National Park is created by Congress.
1927	The Moffat Tunnel under the Rocky Mountains is completed.
1932	A five-year drought begins destroying farms in eastern Colorado.
1947	The Alva B. Adams Tunnel for irrigation is opened.
1959	The series of dams, reservoirs, and tunnels that make up the Colorado-Big Thompson system is completed.
1966	The North American Air Defense Command begins combat operations in Cheyenne Mountain.
1977	The Solar Energy Research Institute is opened near Denver.
1988	More than 1.5 million acres of land is destroyed by drought.
1992	Colorado's first Native American United States senator, Ben Nighthorse Campbell, is elected.

The red letter *C* on the flag stands for Colorado. The gold in the center of the letter symbolizes the gold strikes during the 1800s. The blue and white stripes stand for the blue sky and the snowcapped mountains.

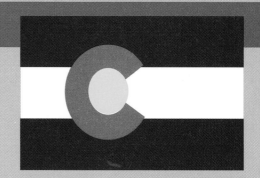

Colorado Almanac

State Bird. Lark bunting

State Flower. Rocky Mountain columbine

State Tree. Blue spruce

State Motto. *Nil sine Numine* (Nothing Without Providence)

State Song. "Where the Columbine Grows"

State Abbreviations. Colo. (traditional); CO (postal)

Statehood. August 1, 1876, the 38th state

Government. Congress: U.S. senators, 2; U.S. representatives, 6. State legislature: senators, 35; representatives, 65. Counties: 63

Area. 104,091 sq mi (269,595 sq km), 8th in size among the states.

Greatest Distances. north/south, 276 mi (444 km); east/west, 387 mi (623 km)

Elevation. Highest: Mount Elbert, 14,433 ft (4,399 m). Lowest: 3,350 ft (1,021 m), along the Arkansas River

Population. 1990 Census: 3,307,912 (14.5% increase over 1980), 26th among the states. Density: 31.9 persons per sq mi (12.3 persons per sq km). Distribution: 80.6% urban, 19.4% rural. 1980 Census: 2,888,834

Economy. *Agriculture:* beef cattle, wheat, corn, dairy products, hay, hogs and pigs, potatoes, sugar beets, apples, onions. *Manufacturing:* scientific instruments, medical equipment, food processing (meat products, beer, soft drinks, animal feeds), nonelectrical machinery, computers, consumer electronics. *Mining:* petroleum, natural gas, coal, molybdenum, limestone, sand, gravel, gold, silver, uranium

State Seal

State Flower:
Rocky Mountain columbine

State Bird: Lark bunting

Annual Events

★ New Year's Eve fireworks on Pikes Peak

★ National Western Stock Show in Denver (January)

★ Winter Carnival in Steamboat Springs (February)

★ World Cup Ski Racing in Aspen and Vail (February and March)

★ Wine Festival and Balloon Rally in Telluride (June)

★ Pikes Peak Auto Race (July)

★ Aspen Music Festival (July and August)

★ Colorado State Fair in Pueblo (August)

★ Pikes Peak or Bust Rodeo in Colorado Springs (August)

★ Larimer Square Oktoberfest in Denver (September and October)

★ Dog Sled Racing in Leadville (December)

Places to Visit

★ Bent's Old Fort, east of La Junta

★ Buffalo Bill's Grave on Lookout Mountain, near Golden

★ Crow Canyon Archaeological Center, west of Cortez

★ Dinosaur National Monument, west of Craig

★ Garden of the Gods, near Colorado Springs

★ Great Sand Dunes National Monument, near Alamosa

★ Mesa Verde National Park, southeast of Cortez

★ Narrow Gauge Railroad, between Durango and Silverton

★ Pikes Peak, west of Colorado Springs

★ Rocky Mountain National Park, near Estes Park, northwest of Denver

★ Royal Gorge, near Canon City

★ U.S. Mint in Denver

Index